MUSIC THERAPY BENEFITS

Complete Guide To Music Therapy Transforms Psychological, Cognitive, Physical, Social, And Emotional Well-Being: Insights, Case Studies, And Practical Strategies

WILFREDO CARSON

INTRODUCTION 3

CHAPTER 1 ....**13**

OVERVIEW OF MUSIC THERAPY.................................13

CHAPTER 2 ....**22**

MUSIC'S PSYCHOLOGICAL EFFECT 22

CHAPTER 3 ....**27**

HEALTHCARE MUSIC THERAPY 27

CHAPTER 4 ....**32**

MUSIC THERAPY AND COGNITIVE BENEFITS.................32

CHAPTER 5 ....**41**

PHYSICAL BENEFITS OF MUSIC THERAPY 41

CHAPTER 6 ....**59**

SOCIAL AND EMOTIONAL BENEFITS 59

CHAPTER 7 ....**73**

CASE STUDIES 73

CHAPTER 8 ....**82**

INCORPORATING MUSIC THERAPY INTO DAILY LIFE....82

CHAPTER 9 ....**88**

CHALLENGES AND ETHICAL CONSIDERATIONS............88

CONCLUSION 93

INTRODUCTION

Music therapy is a growing discipline in healthcare and psychology that uses music to heal and improve well-being. This extensive study examines music therapy's many facets to understand its remarkable effects on people of all backgrounds. This conversation examines music therapy's aim, definition, and history to demonstrate its transforming power and ongoing significance in healthcare.

Purpose of Book:

The main goal of this book is to analyze music therapy's many benefits and uses. We want to understand music therapists' concepts and ambitions by examining their purpose.

The wide range of uses for music therapy, from emotional expression to cognitive development, shows its versatility.

Reading the chapters will help readers understand how music therapy improves physical, emotional, and psychological health.

<u>Music therapy definition:</u>

Defining music therapy is difficult because it involves several methods. Music therapy is the clinical and evidence-based use of music therapies to achieve therapeutic aims in a therapeutic partnership. Music therapy is professional and integrated into healthcare practices, as this definition shows. We shall examine the principles and frameworks that characterize music therapy throughout the book to distinguish it from recreational or casual musical activities.

Music Therapy History:

Music therapy's history must be studied to understand its current state. The history of music therapy shows its development and the cultural and societal conditions that shaped it. This section examines key milestones and influential figures who helped establish and grow music therapy as a discipline, from ancient civilizations recognizing music's healing power to the 20th century's formalization. Appreciating music therapy's current importance in many therapeutic settings requires understanding this historical backdrop.

The Healing Power of Music:

Music therapy works because of its healing qualities. Rhythm, melody, harmony, and timbre are examples.

Each factor affects music's emotional, cognitive, and physiological effects.

To achieve therapeutic purposes, music therapists intentionally use these elements. Melody can evoke emotions and help self-expression, while rhythm can control and synchronize physical activities. Readers will discover how music may be a great healing tool by exploring these characteristics.

<u>Music Therapy Psychological Mechanisms:</u>

The psychological mechanisms that make music therapy successful are complex and linked to human cognition and emotion.

Music affects attention, memory, and executive functioning, making it a therapeutic tool for dementia and neurodevelopmental problems. Music can also improve mood, reduce stress, and express emotions.

These psychological mechanisms will reveal how music therapy affects the mind, enabling tailored and evidence-based interventions.

<u>Physiological Effects of Music Therapy:</u>

Besides its psychological effects, music therapy has several physiological effects.

These responses—from heart rate and blood pressure changes to dopamine and oxytocin release—help the therapeutic impact.

Tailoring music therapy to individual health situations requires understanding its physiological underpinnings. Music therapy's physiological aspects demonstrate its holistic approach to well-being, whether used for pain management, rehabilitation, or stress reduction.

<u>Clinical Uses of Music Therapy:</u>

Music therapy is versatile and adaptable, with uses in many clinical contexts. Music therapy treats depression, anxiety, and PTSD in mental health settings. It is crucial to physical and motor skill development in neurological injury therapy. Music therapy improves communication and development in children. Music therapy's many applications demonstrate its versatility, making it a valuable healthcare tool.

Music Therapy for Special Populations:

Music therapy is notable for its capacity to serve particular populations with distinct needs and obstacles. This section discusses music therapy in children, geriatrics, and neurodevelopmental disorders. Music therapy is person-centered and inclusive since it may be tailored to each population.

Case studies and empirical evidence will demonstrate how music therapy improves quality of life across the lifespan and meets the demands of varied communities.

<u>Cultural Competence in Music Therapy:</u>

Music therapy, which emphasizes human expression and cultural diversity, requires a comprehensive grasp of cultural competence. This involves acknowledging and respecting clients' cultures, adapting therapies to cultural preferences, and creating an inclusive, culturally sensitive therapeutic setting.

The ethical issues and challenges of culturally appropriate music therapy are examined. Readers will learn how cultural competence maximizes music therapy effectiveness across varied groups by studying real-world examples and best practices.

Music therapy research and evidence-based practice

The validity and expansion of any therapy method depend on robust research and evidence-based approaches. This section critically reviews music therapy studies, emphasizing the necessity for robust methods and empirical evidence to prove its usefulness. Readers will grasp music therapy research by reviewing significant papers and meta-analyses. This part also discusses research difficulties and opportunities, advancing the field and integrating music therapy into evidence-based healthcare practices.

Music Therapy Ethics and Professional Development:

As a growing field, music therapy values professional development and ethics.

This section covers the music therapist's educational and certification path. Readers will learn about ethical decision-making and professional conduct from the profession's code of ethics. Music therapists must maintain professional development to stay current and deliver high-quality, ethical care to their clients.

This comprehensive study of music therapy covers its goal, definition, history, therapeutic features, psychological mechanisms, physiological reactions, clinical applications, and cultural competence. The book explores music therapy's distinctive contributions to specific populations, research, and evidence-based approaches, ending with professional growth and ethics. Music therapy's transforming potential shines as a beacon of hope and healing, improving healthcare and psychology with its harmonious resonance. These principles aim to provide readers with a deep grasp of music therapy and inspire a continued appreciation for its role in well-being and human connection.

CHAPTER 1
OVERVIEW OF MUSIC THERAPY

Music therapy is a growing field that uses music to treat physical, emotional, cognitive, and social issues. It is a well-established allied health profession that uses music to achieve therapeutic aims and improve well-being. Music therapy understands that music may move people beyond linguistic barriers and tap into the universal human experience.

Role of Music Therapist

Music therapists are crucial. These specialists combine their music and psychology skills to personalize solutions to their customers' requirements. Music therapists treat developmental difficulties, mental health issues, and physical limitations in children, adults, and the elderly.

They tailor their methods to customer preferences and therapeutic aims.

Music Therapy Methods

1.3.1 Active Music Therapy

Active music therapy involves making music. Clients play instruments, sing, and do rhythmic exercises to make music. This hands-on method encourages self-expression, emotional release, and fine and gross motor skills. Motor coordination, communication, and social interaction benefit most from active music therapy. The therapist tailors activities to the client's needs to foster active engagement and self-expression.

1.3.2 Receptive Music Therapy

Receptive music therapy uses music for therapy, unlike active music therapy.

The therapist guides clients through pre-recorded or live music to attain therapeutic aims. This modality uses music's emotional and psychological power to solve problems. Receptive music therapy can target cognitive functions like memory attention and emotional well-being to help people control their emotions through unique musical experiences.

1.3.3 Creative Music Therapy

Creative music therapy involves improvisation and flexibility. Clients are encouraged to experiment with different musical elements without traditional musical structures.

This form of self-expression allows for spontaneous expression and can help those who struggle with spoken communication. The therapist helps clients experiment with sounds, rhythms, and melodies in a secure environment. Creative music therapy can be used for developmental difficulties, trauma survivors, and stress and anxiety sufferers.

Developmental Disorders and Music Therapy

Music therapy is effective for developmental disorders like autism spectrum disorder.

For ASD patients, who thrive on regularity and repetition, music's structure and predictability can bring stability and comfort. Active music therapy with rhythm and melody helps improve motor coordination and communication in developmental delays. Receptive music therapy, which emphasizes listening and emotional expression, helps improve social skills and emotional regulation in this population.

Music Therapy for Mental Health

Music therapy is an effective supplement to established mental health therapies. Active and receptive music therapy can help depression, anxiety, and PTSD sufferers. Receptive music therapy allows non-intrusive emotional exploration and processing, while active music-making activities relieve stress. Music's rhythms and melodies help soothe the nervous system and improve mental health.

What Music Therapy Does to Cognitive Function

Music therapy improves cognitive function, making it useful in treating dementia and Alzheimer's disease. Musical exercises with rhythm and repetition can improve memory, attention, and executive function due to their structure.

With well-chosen music, receptive music therapy can stimulate memories and emotions, making it meaningful and delightful. Beyond the elderly, music therapy can help traumatic brain injury and other cognitive impairment patients.

Pain Management Using Music Therapy

Music therapy can relieve pain without drugs. Music can relieve medical worry, divert from pain, and relax people. Active music therapy, including playing a musical instrument or doing rhythmic exercises, might distract from pain. In clinical settings, receptive music therapy can release endorphins and give a comprehensive approach to pain management.

The Social Impact of Music Therapy

The power of music therapy to develop social bonds and community is unique. In schools, community centers, and hospitals, group music therapy sessions allow people to collaborate and share their musical experiences. Autism and social anxiety sufferers benefit from this social aspect. Music therapy improves communication, turn-taking, and cooperation, building social relationships and belonging.

Cultural Music Therapy Considerations

Culturally sensitive music therapy is essential for its efficacy and relevance across varied communities. Therapists must understand their clients' cultures since music is profoundly ingrained. Using culturally appropriate music and instruments increases the therapeutic process and creates familiarity. Music therapy also helps people from diverse cultures communicate and bond.

Music Therapy Research and Evidence

Music therapy is always evolving, with research proving its benefits. Many studies have examined music therapy's effects on different demographics and conditions, adding to its evidence base. Music therapy research uses quantitative methods like controlled clinical trials and qualitative methods to capture patients' subjective experiences. Evidence shows that music therapy has several benefits, making it a beneficial treatment modality.

Music therapy is a powerful and adaptable treatment that improves many groups and ailments. Music therapy improves well-being and quality of life for developmental disabilities, mental health issues, cognitive impairments, and pain management.

The music therapist is crucial, using psychology and music to personalize interventions to each patient's needs. As knowledge grows, music therapy may be integrated into conventional healthcare to promote holistic, person-centered healing and wellness.

CHAPTER 2
MUSIC'S PSYCHOLOGICAL EFFECT

Music evokes a range of emotions and shapes mental processes. This impact is largely due to music and emotions. From joy and enthusiasm to grief and nostalgia, music may evoke many emotions. Individuals' responses to tempo, melody, and harmony reflect their psychological constitution and emotional resonance. Understanding how music affects emotions is essential to its therapeutic potential. This research analyses the subtle ways different genres, tones, and rhythms can evoke emotions, helping music therapists tailor interventions to individual emotional needs.

Music's enormous effect on the human psyche is revealed by studying its neurological underpinnings. The brain processes music in a complicated way, engaging emotion, memory, and reward centers, according to neuroscience. Music perception is emotional and cognitive due to the auditory cortex, limbic system, and frontal cortex's complex interaction. Understanding these neurological pathways illuminates music's brain effects and provides a framework for tailored therapeutic interventions. Neuroimaging techniques are improving, allowing researchers to study the neurological mechanisms of music perception and develop more complex music therapy applications.

Memory development and retrieval are other important psychological effect of music.

Some songs or melodies trigger memories of specific events or emotions.

This phenomenon has been used to treat memory problems like Alzheimer's. Music therapy uses individualized playlists or musical cues to improve memory recall and cognition. Exploring how music aids memory processes can improve and broaden music therapy for memory-related issues in varied populations.

Music helps promote mental health by reducing stress. Numerous studies have shown that music lowers cortisol, heart rate, and subjective stress. Music can help reduce stress in clinical and daily settings. Music therapists can create personalized interventions by understanding how tempo, rhythm, and timbre reduce stress.

Music therapy in holistic stress management may improve resilience and mental health as stress-related problems continue to plague mental health.

The dynamic relationship between music and mood permeates music therapy. This research examines how musical aspects, genres, and structures affect mood. Music is a flexible instrument for mood control and enhancement since it can cause instant and prolonged mood shifts. Understanding this relationship helps music therapists target mood disorders and swings with music therapies. Whether to raise and energize depressed people or calm and soothe anxious people, music selection and use are crucial to emotional well-being therapies.

In music therapy, emotions, neurological processes, memory dynamics, stress modulation, and mood management interact. The degree of understanding in each domain improves music therapy approaches. Continued research will reveal new aspects of music's therapeutic potential, expanding doctors' and practitioners' mental health and well-being tools.

CHAPTER 3
HEALTHCARE MUSIC THERAPY

Music therapy has been shown to improve patient's overall health in numerous healthcare settings. Music therapy is part of comprehensive hospital care for patients with various medical disorders. Hospital music therapy includes evidence-based interventions for physical, emotional, and cognitive well-being. Hospital music therapists collaborate with doctors to include music in patient-specific therapy plans. We work together to improve patient care and health outcomes.

Hospital Music Therapy

Music therapy is used in many medical departments and specialties to treat many health issues.

Music reduces pain without medication, which is a major benefit. Music reduces pain perception and promotes relaxation, making it a useful pain management tool, according to numerous researches. Music therapy helps patients express themselves and release emotions, boosting emotional well-being. Chronic illness patients typically struggle with psychological issues. Hospital patients may benefit from active music-making, listening sessions, and lyric analysis.

<u>Palliative Music Therapy</u>

In palliative care, music therapy improves the quality of life for those with life-limiting illnesses. Music therapy addresses physical, emotional, social, and spiritual issues holistically.

Music therapy helps palliative patients and their families feel connected and meaningful.

Music therapists work with interdisciplinary healthcare teams to create individualized interventions. Live music, songwriting, and music-assisted relaxation can create a therapeutic setting that fosters calm and dignity during end-of-life.

<u>Music Therapy in Mental Health</u>

Music therapy is becoming acknowledged as a valuable and diverse remedy for a variety of mental health issues. Music therapy in mental health addresses emotional expression, social interaction, and cognition. Therapy using music gives people who struggle to express themselves a nonverbal outlet. Music therapists help clients explore emotions, self-awareness, and coping skills in psychiatric hospitals and outpatient mental health programs. The collaborative element of music therapy builds community and connection, helping heal sadness, anxiety, and trauma.

<u>Therapeutic Music for Special Needs Kids</u>

Special needs children may struggle with speech, socializing, and physical abilities. These issues can be addressed with developmentally appropriate and engaging music therapy. Music therapists work with interdisciplinary teams to help children with developmental impairments, autism spectrum disorders, and neurological illnesses.

Music therapy is creative and dynamic, adapted to each child's needs and talents. Instrument play, singing, and music-based movement promote communication, fine and gross motor skills, and social skills in youngsters.

Music can help special needs children succeed due to its excitement and inspiration.

Music therapy in healthcare has several uses that improve people's health and well-being. Music therapy is an effective, evidence-based intervention for physical, emotional, and social health in hospitals, palliative care, mental health, and pediatric care. Music therapists and healthcare professionals work together to improve patients' quality of life.

Music therapy's role in holistic healthcare will grow as research and practice progress.

CHAPTER 4
MUSIC THERAPY AND COGNITIVE BENEFITS

Cognitive development is greatly impacted by music therapy. Music boosts cognitive processes. Music and memory are linked, especially in Alzheimer's and dementia.

Music therapy triggers memories and emotions by tapping into cognitive reserves. Music therapy also improves learning across varied populations, supporting its cognitive benefits.

Cognitive Development and Music

Scholars study music and cognitive development. Music helps youngsters improve cognitive skills by engaging numerous brain processes.

Early music exposure improves memory, attention, and executive functioning, according to research. Learning to play a musical instrument integrates sensory and motor skills, increasing cognitive development and boosting brain connections. The rhythmic and melodic parts of music can also stimulate language processing and mathematical reasoning areas, improving cognitive skills.

Alzheimer's and dementia music therapy

Music therapy can help Alzheimer's and dementia patients' cognitive abilities. Memory loss, perplexity, and emotional anguish are common in these diseases. The emotional and cognitive links to music that survive even in advanced stages of many disorders make music therapy powerful. Therapists can help

Alzheimer's and dementia patients recall memories, reduce anxiety, and improve cognitive function with individualized playlists and music. Music can preserve cognition beyond immediate sessions, making it helpful.

Using Music to Improve Learning Music has been used to improve learning in schools. Music therapy uses the brain's natural relationship to music to teach. Music in learning contexts improves memory, attention, and problem-solving, according to research. The rhythmic and melodic patterns in music can help you remember information.

The success of music therapy in special education shows its adaptability to varied learning demands. The multidimensional approach to boosting learning through music shows its promise in education.

Music Therapy for Emotional Health

Music Expresses Emotion

Music therapy helps people express their emotions nonverbally. Music helps customers express and process difficult feelings.

This is important in therapeutic settings where people with psychological illnesses or trauma may have trouble speaking. Through improvisation, song writing, or pre-existing music, clients can express and explore many emotions. Music enhances the client-therapist interaction by developing trust and allowing emotional expression in a safe and supportive atmosphere.

Musical Therapy for Mental Health

Music therapy is a beneficial mental health supplement. It supplements standard therapy by addressing emotional, cognitive, and social mental health.

Making and listening to music can help people express and process complex emotions. Depression, anxiety, and trauma are treated by music therapy. Music therapy interventions are structured but adaptable, allowing therapists to tailor sessions to each patient's needs, improving mental health treatment.

<u>Reduce Stress and Relax with Music</u>

A major use of music therapy is stress reduction and relaxation. The physiological and psychological effects of music on stress have been extensively explored.

Calming music, music-based relaxation techniques, and guided music visualization help reduce stress hormones and stress-related physical symptoms. Music therapy helps people manage stress in clinical and everyday settings. The power of music to modify emotions and promote relaxation makes it a promising non-pharmacological stress management and well-being tool.

Social and Communication Benefits of Music Therapy

<u>Autism Spectrum Disorder Music Therapy</u>

Music therapy has helped autistic people with social and communication issues. Autism sufferers find music predictable and fascinating due to its structure and rhythm. Music therapy improves socialization, communication, and emotional expression in a safe, supportive environment. Instruments, songs, and rhythmic activities can help autistic people learn and practice social skills, improving relationships and quality of life.

Enhancing Social Skills with Group Music Therapy

Group music therapy is a dynamic way to build social skills and relationships. Group music-making encourages cooperation, turn-taking, and communication. This is especially helpful for people with developmental, psychological, or neurological issues who struggle with social interactions. Group music therapy provides a structured but flexible space for people to share musical experiences and develop social skills in a supportive environment. Collective music-making fosters community and social well-being.

Music Therapy for Communication Disorders

Communication disorders affect people throughout their lives. Music therapy can address these issues by using music's communicative power.

Therapists use music-based interventions to improve speech articulation, language comprehension, and nonverbal communication. Music's rhythm and melody can help people with communication disorders practice and improve. Music therapy inspires expression and connection in people who struggle with language.

Music therapy is a complex intervention that benefits cognitive, emotional, and social domains. The cognitive benefits of music therapy are evident in its impact on cognitive development, its application in Alzheimer's and dementia care, and its role in enhancing learning outcomes. The emotional well-being facilitated by music therapy encompasses emotional expression, mental health treatment, and stress reduction. Lastly, the social and communication benefits of music therapy extend to diverse populations, including individuals with autism spectrum disorder, those seeking enhanced social skills, and those addressing communication disorders.

As a holistic and adaptable therapeutic approach, music therapy continues to evolve, making significant contributions to the well-being and quality of life of individuals across various contexts and stages of life.

CHAPTER 5
PHYSICAL BENEFITS OF MUSIC THERAPY

Music therapy has demonstrated significant physical benefits across various domains, contributing to the overall well-being of individuals. In the realm of rehabilitation music therapy has emerged as a powerful adjunct to conventional therapies. Patients recovering from surgeries, injuries, or debilitating conditions find solace and motivation through structured musical interventions. Therapists strategically use rhythm, melody, and harmony to engage individuals in exercises that promote muscle strength, coordination, and flexibility.

The rhythmic elements of music, in particular, provide a rhythmic cue for movement, aiding in the restoration of impaired motor functions.

The role of music therapy in pain management cannot be overstated. It offers a non-pharmacological approach to alleviating pain, particularly in chronic conditions.

The emotional and psychological impact of music contributes to a reduction in the perception of pain, creating a more positive and relaxed state. This has implications for individuals suffering from conditions such as fibromyalgia, arthritis, or post-surgical pain. Through personalized musical interventions, therapists tailor experiences to address specific pain triggers, facilitating a holistic approach to pain management that extends beyond pharmaceutical interventions.

Another facet of physical benefits involves the enhancement of motor skills through music therapy. This is particularly evident in populations dealing with neurological disorders such as stroke survivors or individuals with Parkinson's disease. Music therapy taps into the brain's plasticity, utilizing musical stimuli to stimulate neural pathways associated with motor functions.

Rhythmic auditory cues in music assist in regulating and improving gait, coordination, and overall motor control. This application extends to pediatric populations as well, where music therapy is utilized to enhance motor skills development in children with developmental delays.

Emotional Benefits of Music Therapy

Beyond its physical impacts, music therapy profoundly influences emotional well-being, providing individuals with a powerful outlet for expression and exploration.

This therapeutic modality has been instrumental in fostering emotional resilience, enabling individuals to navigate and cope with various emotional challenges.

In the context of emotional expression music therapy offers a unique platform for individuals to communicate and articulate complex emotions that may be difficult to express verbally. Through musical improvisation, lyric analysis, or song writing, individuals can explore and process their emotional experiences in a safe and supportive environment. This is particularly beneficial for those dealing with trauma, grief, or emotional distress, as it provides an alternative avenue for expression beyond traditional talk therapy.

Music therapy's impact on mood regulation is evident in its ability to induce emotional responses and evoke specific feelings. Therapists strategically select musical elements such as tempo, pitch, and dynamics to elicit desired emotional states.

This approach is harnessed in various clinical settings, from alleviating symptoms of depression and anxiety to enhancing overall emotional well-being. The use of music as a mood modulator extends to populations dealing with mood disorders, providing a complementary therapeutic approach to conventional treatments.

Additionally, music therapy plays a pivotal role in promoting emotional self-awareness Through engaging in musical activities and reflecting on the emotional content of musical experiences, individuals gain insight into their emotional states and triggers. This heightened self-awareness becomes a valuable tool in developing emotional intelligence and fostering a deeper understanding of one's emotional landscape. In therapeutic settings, this aspect of music therapy is particularly valuable for individuals navigating interpersonal challenges or seeking personal growth.

<u>Cognitive Benefits of Music Therapy</u>

The cognitive benefits of music therapy extend across a spectrum of domains, showcasing its efficacy in enhancing cognitive functions, promoting neuroplasticity, and addressing cognitive challenges in diverse populations.

In the realm of cognitive rehabilitation music therapy has demonstrated remarkable effectiveness in supporting individuals with cognitive impairments resulting from conditions such as traumatic brain injury, dementia, or neurodevelopmental disorders. Structured musical activities engage various cognitive processes, including attention, memory, and executive functions. Therapists utilize musical interventions to create tailored exercises that challenge and stimulate cognitive abilities, promoting neural connectivity and cognitive recovery.

Music therapy's impact on memory enhancement has been the subject of extensive research. Particularly in individuals with Alzheimer's disease and other forms of dementia, music has shown the ability to evoke memories and stimulate cognitive functions. The emotional and autobiographical connections tied to music provide a unique pathway for accessing and preserving memories. Therapists leverage this phenomenon by incorporating personalized playlists or musical reminiscence activities, tapping into the power of music to enhance memory recall and cognitive functioning.

Furthermore, music therapy catalyzes neuroplasticity (7.3), the brain's capacity to reorganize and adapt. In neurological rehabilitation, this property is harnessed to facilitate recovery and improve cognitive functions. Music engages multiple regions of the brain simultaneously, promoting the formation of new neural connections.

This is particularly valuable in cases of stroke or neurodegenerative diseases, where the brain's ability to rewire itself can contribute to functional recovery and adaptation.

<u>Social Benefits of Music Therapy</u>

The social benefits of music therapy underscore its capacity to foster connections, enhance social skills, and promote a sense of belonging within diverse populations. Through group interventions and tailored activities, music therapy becomes a powerful tool for building and strengthening social relationships.

In the realm of interpersonal communication (8.1), music therapy offers a unique avenue for individuals with communication challenges to express themselves and connect with others. This is particularly evident in populations such as children with autism spectrum disorder (ASD) or individuals with communication disorders.

Music provides a structured and non-threatening medium for communication, allowing individuals to interact and express themselves in ways that may be challenging through conventional verbal communication. Therapists employ musical activities to enhance communication skills, promote social interaction, and cultivate meaningful connections.

The group dynamics inherent in music therapy contribute to the development of social skills (8.2). In both paediatric and adult populations, engaging in musical activities within a group setting fosters teamwork, cooperation, and a sense of community. Therapists design interventions that require collaboration, turn-taking, and mutual support, creating opportunities for individuals to develop and practice essential social skills.

This is particularly valuable for populations facing social challenges, such as individuals with social anxiety or those on the autism spectrum.

Moreover, music therapy plays a pivotal role in building a sense of community and belonging (8.3). In diverse settings, from healthcare institutions to community programs, group music-making experiences create a shared sense of purpose and connection. This communal aspect of music therapy contributes to the development of a supportive environment, where individuals feel understood, accepted, and valued.

This is especially relevant in populations facing isolation or marginalization, as music therapy becomes a means of fostering a sense of belonging and inclusion.

Spiritual Benefits of Music Therapy

The spiritual dimension of music therapy encompasses its capacity to facilitate a connection with the inner self, promote existential exploration, and contribute to a sense of purpose and meaning in life.

This aspect of music therapy transcends religious affiliations, focusing on the broader exploration of spirituality as a fundamental aspect of human experience.

In the realm of existential exploration music therapy provides individuals with a space for contemplation and reflection on life's profound questions. Through musical improvisation, lyric analysis, or guided imagery with music, therapists guide individuals in exploring existential themes such as purpose, identity, and life's meaning. This introspective process fosters a deeper understanding of one's values and beliefs, contributing to a sense of coherence and purpose in the face of life's challenges.

The therapeutic use of music in promoting mindfulness and meditation (9.2) aligns with the spiritual dimension of music therapy. Mindfulness practices, often integrated into music therapy sessions, encourage individuals to be present in the moment and cultivate a heightened awareness of their thoughts and emotions. Music serves as a meditative anchor, guiding individuals into a state of mindfulness that transcends the immediate therapeutic setting. This integration of music and mindfulness contributes to stress reduction, enhanced emotional regulation, and an overall sense of spiritual well-being.

Moreover, music therapy plays a role in facilitating transcendent experiences (9.3) that go beyond the mundane aspects of daily life. This can be particularly impactful for individuals facing existential challenges, such as those dealing with terminal illnesses or navigating the complexities of grief. Through carefully curated musical experiences, therapists create a space for individuals to connect with a sense of transcendence, providing solace, comfort, and a broader perspective on their life journey.

Educational Benefits of Music Therapy

In the educational context, music therapy serves as a dynamic and effective tool for enhancing academic and developmental outcomes. By leveraging the inherent engaging qualities of music, therapists address a range of educational goals, from academic achievement to social-emotional development.

Academic achievement is positively influenced by the incorporation of music therapy in educational settings. Numerous studies have shown that music can enhance cognitive functions related to learning, such as memory, attention, and problem-solving skills. Music therapy interventions are designed to align with educational objectives, utilizing rhythm, melody, and lyrics to reinforce academic content. This approach proves particularly beneficial for individuals with learning disabilities, as the multisensory nature of music engages various modalities, accommodating diverse learning styles.

The use of music therapy in promoting social skills in educational settings is also noteworthy. In classrooms, music becomes a powerful tool for fostering teamwork, communication, and cooperation.

Group music-making activities provide a structured platform for students to interact, share ideas, and collaborate on creative projects. This collaborative aspect of music therapy contributes to the development of social-emotional skills, enhancing students' ability to navigate social relationships and work effectively in group settings.

Additionally, music therapy supports the development of emotional intelligence and self-regulation in educational contexts.

By incorporating music into social-emotional learning programs, therapists help students explore and understand their emotions. Musical activities provide a non-threatening medium for self-expression and reflection, promoting emotional awareness and regulation. This, in turn, contributes to a positive and supportive learning environment where students feel empowered to navigate their emotions and interpersonal relationships.

the multifaceted benefits of music therapy underscore its versatility as a therapeutic modality. From the physical realm of rehabilitation and pain management to the emotional and cognitive domains of expression, memory enhancement, and cognitive rehabilitation, music therapy offers a holistic approach to addressing diverse health and well-being needs. Its social applications in communication, social skill development, and community-building highlight its capacity to foster meaningful connections.

Additionally, the spiritual dimension of music therapy contributes to existential exploration, mindfulness, and transcendent experiences.

In educational settings, music therapy emerges as a valuable tool for academic achievement, social skill development, and emotional intelligence. The integration of music into therapeutic interventions showcases its potential to enhance the overall quality of life across various populations. As research continues to unravel the intricacies of music's impact on the human mind and body, music therapy stands as a dynamic and evolving field with profound implications for healthcare, education, and the broader spectrum of human experience.

CHAPTER 6
SOCIAL AND EMOTIONAL BENEFITS

Music therapy is a holistic approach that encompasses a wide range of benefits, particularly in the realms of social and emotional well-being. One of the key facets of this therapeutic modality is the enhancement of social skills through musical interactions.

In a therapeutic setting, individuals are encouraged to engage in musical activities that promote communication, cooperation, and collaboration. This is particularly impactful for individuals with social difficulties, such as those on the autism spectrum or individuals with social anxiety disorders. The structured and non-threatening nature of musical interactions allows participants to develop and practice social skills in a supportive environment. For example, group drumming sessions may require participants to synchronize their beats, fostering a sense of teamwork and mutual understanding.

Moreover, music therapy serves as a powerful medium for expressing emotions. Music can evoke and elicit a wide range of emotions, and therapists leverage this capacity to help individuals explore and articulate their feelings. Through musical improvisation, composition, or simply listening to carefully curated playlists, individuals can navigate and process complex emotions. This is particularly relevant in cases of trauma, grief, or mental health disorders where verbal expression may be challenging. The therapeutic relationship between the client and the music therapist facilitates a safe space for emotional exploration, allowing individuals to express themselves in ways that may be difficult through traditional talk therapy.

Additionally, music therapy in group settings offers unique advantages for social and emotional development. Group therapy sessions provide a platform for individuals to connect with others who may share similar experiences or challenges. The shared musical experience becomes a common ground, fostering a sense of belonging and community. In group settings, participants have the opportunity to witness and support each other's emotional expression, creating a supportive and empathetic environment. This communal aspect of music therapy is particularly beneficial for individuals struggling with isolation or feelings of disconnectedness. Group music-making activities, such as ensemble performances or collaborative songwriting, further contribute to a sense of shared achievement and camaraderie.

<u>Cognitive Benefits</u>

Beyond social and emotional benefits, music therapy has been recognized for its profound impact on cognitive functions. The intricate relationship between music and the brain has led to the development of therapeutic interventions aimed at enhancing various cognitive abilities. Music therapy serves as a cognitive stimulant, engaging different areas of the brain involved in memory, attention, and executive functions. Engaging in musical activities, such as learning to play an instrument or participating in rhythm-based exercises, can contribute to improved cognitive functioning.

A notable application of music therapy is in memory improvement. Music has a unique ability to evoke memories and associations due to its strong connections with emotional experiences. In the context of dementia or other memory-related disorders, music therapy has shown promising results.

Familiar tunes from the past can elicit memories and emotions, providing individuals with a sense of connection and continuity. Therapists often use personalized playlists or live music interventions to stimulate memory recall and create meaningful experiences for individuals with cognitive impairments.

Moreover, music therapy has demonstrated therapeutic efficacy in neurological disorders such as Parkinson's disease and stroke. Rhythmic auditory stimulation, a technique involving the use of rhythmic auditory cues to improve movement and gait, has been widely employed in the rehabilitation of individuals with Parkinson's disease. The rhythmic elements of music help regulate movement patterns and enhance motor coordination. Similarly, melodic intonation therapy has been utilized to facilitate speech recovery in individuals with aphasia following a stroke. These applications highlight the neuroplasticity-inducing effects of music therapy, showcasing its potential to enhance cognitive and motor functions in individuals with neurological challenges.

<u>Psychological Benefits</u>

Music therapy plays a significant role in promoting psychological well-being by addressing issues related to anxiety, stress, and trauma. The therapeutic use of music has been shown to have a calming and soothing effect on the nervous system, making it a valuable tool in the reduction of anxiety and stress. Listening to calming music, engaging in rhythmic activities, or participating in guided relaxation exercises can activate the parasympathetic nervous system, promoting a sense of relaxation and reducing physiological markers of stress.

In the context of trauma recovery, music therapy offers a unique avenue for processing and coping with traumatic experiences. Trauma can often be stored in the body, and traditional talk therapy may not be sufficient to address the somatic aspects of trauma. Music therapy provides a non-verbal means of expression, allowing individuals to release and process traumatic emotions through music. Therapists may incorporate elements of improvisation, song writing, or guided music listening to help individuals explore and integrate their traumatic experiences in a safe and supportive environment.

Furthermore, music therapy facilitates self-expression and identity development.

For individuals grappling with issues of self-esteem or a sense of identity, music becomes a medium through which they can authentically express themselves. Whether through creating original music, engaging in lyrical analysis, or exploring various musical genres, individuals can connect with their inner selves and communicate aspects of their identity that may be difficult to articulate verbally. This process of self-expression fosters a sense of empowerment and self-discovery, contributing to positive psychological outcomes.

<u>Physical Benefits</u>

In addition to its psychological and cognitive benefits, music therapy has been recognized for its positive impact on physical well-being. In the realm of pain management, music therapy has been employed as a non-pharmacological intervention to alleviate pain and discomfort. Listening to music with a slow tempo and calming melodies can trigger the release of endorphins, the body's natural painkillers, providing relief for individuals experiencing chronic pain or undergoing medical procedures. The distraction provided by music also helps shift the focus away from pain, reducing the perception of discomfort.

Music therapy plays a crucial role in motor rehabilitation and coordination, particularly in individuals with physical disabilities or those recovering from injuries. Rhythmic auditory stimulation, as mentioned earlier in the context of neurological disorders, is a technique used to improve motor skills and coordination. Engaging in activities such as drumming, dancing, or playing percussion instruments can enhance motor planning and execution. The rhythmic cues provided by music serve as a guide for movement, facilitating improved coordination and physical rehabilitation.

Moreover, music therapy has implications for respiratory and cardiovascular health. Controlled breathing exercises accompanied by musical elements can improve respiratory function and lung capacity. In conditions such as chronic obstructive pulmonary disease (COPD) or asthma, music therapy can be integrated into pulmonary rehabilitation programs to enhance respiratory muscle strength and endurance. Additionally, the use of live or recorded music with specific tempos can influence heart rate and blood pressure, contributing to cardiovascular health.

Advantages for Education and Development. The application of music therapy extends to the realm of education, where it has been employed to enhance academic skills and support overall developmental milestones. In educational settings, music therapy is utilized as a supplementary tool to address academic goals and objectives. For example, incorporating music into learning activities can enhance memory retention and cognitive processing. Mnemonic devices, such as setting information to music or using rhythmic patterns, are employed to aid in the memorization of academic content.

Furthermore, music therapy has been integrated into special education programs to support individuals with developmental delays or learning disabilities.

 The multisensory nature of music engages various sensory modalities, providing a dynamic and inclusive learning experience. Therapists work collaboratively with educators to design music-based interventions that cater to individual learning styles and developmental needs. For children with autism spectrum disorders, music therapy interventions can improve communication skills, social interaction, and sensory processing.

In terms of developmental milestones, music therapy plays a role in supporting the acquisition of essential skills in children. Early interventions incorporating music can enhance language development, motor skills, and social-emotional competencies. Musical activities such as singing, instrument play, and movement-based exercises contribute to a holistic approach to development, fostering a range of skills that are foundational for later academic success and overall well-being.

the multifaceted nature of music therapy encompasses a wide array of benefits across social, emotional, cognitive, psychological, physical, educational, and developmental domains.

The therapeutic application of music is rooted in its ability to engage individuals on a profound level, addressing diverse needs and promoting well-being. Whether in the context of social skills development, cognitive enhancement, psychological healing, physical rehabilitation, or educational support, music therapy stands as a versatile and effective modality. As the field continues to evolve, ongoing research and clinical practice contribute to a deeper understanding of the mechanisms through which music exerts its therapeutic effects, further solidifying its place as a valuable and integrative approach to holistic health and wellness.

CHAPTER 7
CASE STUDIES

Music therapy has shown significant promise as a therapeutic intervention for individuals with autism spectrum disorder (ASD).

In Case Study 1, we delve into the application of music therapy in the context of autism. Individuals with ASD often experience challenges in social communication, emotional regulation, and sensory processing. Music therapy provides a unique avenue for addressing these challenges by harnessing the power of music to engage individuals on multiple levels. Research indicates that music therapy can enhance social skills, improve emotional expression, and contribute to overall well-being in individuals with autism.

The structured and rhythmic nature of music serves as a non-verbal medium through which individuals with autism can express themselves. Case studies have demonstrated how musical activities, such as improvisation and rhythmic exercises, can facilitate communication and social interaction.

Moreover, the predictable and repetitive elements of music can offer a sense of comfort and predictability for individuals with ASD, who may struggle with changes and unpredictability. Music therapy interventions are tailored to individual needs, allowing therapists to adapt their approaches to match the preferences and sensitivities of each client.

Additionally, neuroscientific research has explored the impact of music on the brain, revealing that music therapy can stimulate neural connections and promote neuroplasticity. This is particularly relevant in the context of autism, where atypical neural connectivity is often observed. The integration of music therapy into comprehensive autism intervention programs has shown promising results, with improvements noted in communication skills, emotional regulation, and overall quality of life for individuals on the spectrum.

Case Study 2: Music Therapy in Stroke Rehabilitation

Stroke survivors often face a myriad of physical, cognitive, and emotional challenges during their rehabilitation journey. Case Study 2 examines the application of music therapy in the context of stroke rehabilitation, shedding light on how this therapeutic modality can contribute to the recovery process. Stroke survivors may experience motor deficits, speech impairments, and emotional distress, all of which can be addressed through targeted music therapy interventions.

One of the key benefits of music therapy in stroke rehabilitation is its ability to engage and motivate individuals in their recovery efforts. Rhythmic auditory stimulation, a technique employed in music therapy, involves the use of rhythmic cues to facilitate movement. In the case of stroke survivors with gait disturbances, this technique has been shown to enhance walking abilities and promote a more natural and rhythmic gait pattern. Similarly, music therapy interventions focusing on fine motor skills can aid in the rehabilitation of hand and arm movements, contributing to improved dexterity and functionality.

Beyond the physical aspects of rehabilitation, music therapy also plays a crucial role in addressing cognitive and emotional challenges post-stroke. Cognitive functions such as memory, attention, and executive functioning can be targeted through music-based activities that stimulate various neural pathways. Moreover, music therapy provides a platform for emotional expression and communication, allowing stroke survivors to cope with the emotional toll of their experiences.

Neuroscientific studies have demonstrated the neuroplasticity-inducing effects of music therapy, highlighting its potential to promote brain reorganization and recovery post-stroke. The integration of music therapy into interdisciplinary rehabilitation programs has emerged as a valuable approach, fostering holistic recovery and enhancing the overall well-being of individuals who have experienced a stroke.

Case Study 3: Music Therapy in Anxiety Treatment

Anxiety disorders represent a prevalent mental health concern, impacting individuals across various age groups. In Case Study 3, we explore the application of music therapy as a therapeutic tool in the treatment of anxiety. Music therapy offers a non-invasive and accessible means of addressing anxiety symptoms, providing individuals with a creative outlet for self-expression and emotional regulation.

The therapeutic use of music in anxiety treatment is grounded in the understanding that music can modulate emotions and physiological responses. Through carefully designed interventions, music therapists work to create a calming and supportive environment for individuals experiencing anxiety. Relaxation techniques, such as guided imagery paired with soothing music, contribute to the reduction of stress hormones and promote a sense of relaxation.

Case studies have demonstrated the efficacy of music therapy in various contexts of anxiety, including generalized anxiety disorder, social anxiety, and post-traumatic stress disorder. The personalized nature of music therapy allows therapists to tailor interventions to the specific needs and preferences of each individual, enhancing the therapeutic alliance and treatment outcomes. Musical elements such as tempo, rhythm, and harmony are carefully chosen to elicit desired emotional responses and promote a sense of safety and comfort.

Neuroscientific research has elucidated the neural mechanisms underlying the anxiolytic effects of music therapy. Functional imaging studies have shown alterations in brain activity and connectivity patterns, suggesting that music therapy can influence neural circuits associated with emotion regulation. Furthermore, the engagement of the limbic system, particularly the amygdala, is observed during music therapy sessions, indicating the potential of music to modulate emotional responses.

Incorporating music therapy into the broader spectrum of anxiety treatment approaches provides a holistic and integrative method for addressing both the cognitive and emotional dimensions of anxiety disorders.

The evidence from case studies highlights the versatility of music therapy as an adjunctive therapeutic tool in the comprehensive treatment of anxiety, offering individuals a

creative and empowering pathway toward
improved mental health.

CHAPTER 8
INCORPORATING MUSIC THERAPY INTO DAILY LIFE

Music therapy is a holistic and innovative approach that harnesses the power of music to address various physical, emotional, cognitive, and social needs of individuals. One aspect of integrating music therapy into daily life is its application for relaxation purposes. Music has a profound impact on the human nervous system, influencing physiological responses and promoting a state of relaxation. Through carefully selected music, therapists can modulate tempo, rhythm, and melody to induce a calming effect, reducing stress and anxiety levels. This therapeutic application is particularly beneficial for individuals facing high levels of stress, such as those with chronic illnesses, mental health disorders, or individuals navigating challenging life situations. The utilization of music for relaxation not only provides a temporary escape from stressors but can also contribute to long-term well-being by fostering a more relaxed and resilient mindset.

<u>DIY Music Therapy Techniques</u>

Do-it-yourself (DIY) music therapy techniques empower individuals to actively engage with music in a self-directed manner, offering a sense of agency and control over their well-being. This approach allows individuals to tailor music interventions to their specific needs and preferences. DIY music therapy techniques encompass a wide range of activities, including listening to personalized playlists, creating and playing musical instruments, singing, and songwriting.

These activities are not limited to musical proficiency; rather, they focus on the individual's subjective experience and expression. For example, creating a personalized playlist with favorite songs or those with positive memories can evoke emotions and memories, promoting a sense of connection and joy.

DIY music therapy techniques are versatile, making them accessible for people of all ages and abilities, fostering a sense of autonomy and self-expression in the therapeutic process.

<u>Integrating Music into Self-Care Practices</u>

The integration of music into self-care practices emphasizes the incorporation of musical elements into routine activities, enhancing the overall well-being of individuals.

This concept recognizes that music can serve as a powerful tool in promoting self-awareness, emotional regulation, and stress reduction.

For instance, incorporating calming music into a morning routine or listening to uplifting tunes during a workout can set a positive tone for the day, contributing to improved mood and energy levels. Moreover, integrating music into mindfulness and meditation practices can enhance the depth of the experience, aiding in concentration and relaxation. The deliberate use of music in self-care practices acknowledges the therapeutic potential of sound and rhythm in influencing emotional states and promoting a balanced lifestyle.

By seamlessly integrating music into daily rituals, individuals can harness its benefits sustainably and proactively, creating a harmonious connection between music and self-care.

Overall, the incorporation of music therapy into daily life encompasses diverse approaches that cater to the unique needs and preferences of individuals.

The relaxation aspect of music therapy provides a targeted intervention for stress reduction, leveraging the physiological responses to music to induce a state of calmness. DIY music therapy techniques empower individuals to actively engage with music, fostering a sense of control and self-expression in the therapeutic process. Integrating music into self-care practices recognizes the potential of music to enhance various aspects of well-being, promoting a harmonious connection between music and daily routines. Collectively, these concepts highlight the versatility and accessibility of music therapy as a holistic approach to enhancing mental, emotional, and physical health.

CHAPTER 9
CHALLENGES AND ETHICAL CONSIDERATIONS

Ethical Guidelines for Music Therapists: Ethical considerations are paramount in the field of music therapy, as therapists navigate the delicate terrain of patient well-being, privacy, and consent. Music therapists adhere to a set of ethical guidelines designed to ensure the highest standards of professional conduct. Central to these guidelines is the principle of confidentiality, emphasizing the importance of safeguarding patient information. This involves a delicate balance between maintaining privacy and collaborating with other healthcare professionals to provide comprehensive care. Additionally, therapists must respect the autonomy and agency of their clients, seeking informed consent for interventions and respecting their right to refuse treatment. The ethical guidelines also address issues of cultural sensitivity, emphasizing the importance of understanding diverse musical preferences and traditions to tailor therapeutic interventions accordingly. As music therapy involves emotional expression, therapists must be vigilant in recognizing and addressing potential emotional or psychological distress, always prioritizing the well-being of their clients.

Challenges in Implementing Music Therapy: While the benefits of music therapy are well-established, implementing it in diverse settings presents a range of challenges. One significant hurdle is the variability in individual responses to music, making it challenging to design standardized interventions that cater to everyone's unique needs.

Moreover, integrating music therapy into conventional healthcare settings requires collaboration with other healthcare professionals, necessitating a shift in institutional attitudes and practices. Funding and resource constraints can hinder the widespread adoption of music therapy programs, limiting access for individuals who could benefit. Additionally, measuring the effectiveness of music therapy poses methodological challenges, as the outcomes are often subjective and influenced by various factors. The need for skilled and trained music therapists further compounds the implementation challenges, as there is a shortage of professionals with the necessary expertise. Overcoming these hurdles requires a concerted effort from policymakers, healthcare institutions, and educators to promote the integration of music therapy into mainstream healthcare.

Future Directions in Music Therapy Research: As the field of music therapy continues to evolve, researchers are exploring new avenues to enhance its effectiveness and broaden its applications. Future research endeavors aim to elucidate the neurobiological mechanisms underlying the therapeutic effects of music, providing a deeper understanding of how music influences the brain and body.

Advances in technology offer exciting possibilities for the development of innovative music therapy interventions, such as virtual reality-enhanced experiences or personalized playlists based on individual preferences and therapeutic goals.

The integration of neuroimaging techniques, such as functional magnetic resonance imaging (fMRI) and electroencephalography (EEG), allows researchers to explore the intricate neural processes involved in music perception and its therapeutic impact. Moreover, researchers are delving into the potential of music therapy in addressing specific clinical conditions, such as neurodegenerative disorders and mental health challenges. Future directions also involve exploring the long-term effects of music therapy and its role in preventive healthcare, paving the way for a more comprehensive and evidence-based approach to incorporating music as a therapeutic modality.

CONCLUSION

the multifaceted benefits of music therapy extend beyond mere entertainment, encompassing physical, emotional, and cognitive dimensions. The therapeutic use of music has demonstrated its efficacy in diverse clinical settings, offering a non-invasive and holistic approach to improving overall well-being. From alleviating pain and anxiety to enhancing cognitive function and promoting emotional expression, music therapy stands as a versatile and valuable adjunct to traditional healthcare practices. However, ethical considerations, such as confidentiality and cultural sensitivity, must be diligently addressed to ensure the responsible and effective implementation of music therapy. The challenges in widespread adoption, including variability in individual responses and resource constraints, underscore the need for concerted efforts from policymakers and healthcare institutions. Looking ahead, the future of music therapy research holds promise, with advancements in neuroscience and technology contributing to a deeper understanding of its mechanisms and expanding its applications. As the field continues to evolve, music therapy is poised to play an increasingly integral role in promoting holistic health and well-being for diverse populations.